FRENCH
Decorative Designs

P. PLANAT

DOVER PUBLICATIONS, INC., MINEOLA NEW YORK

Note

These elegant French designs have been selected from *Le Style dans la Peinture Décorative,* a rare, nineteenth-century portfolio filled with colorful borders, ornaments, panels, and wallpapers. P. Planat, a notable contributor to the art and architectural world, was the editor of one of the first major and architectural encyclopedias, *Encyclopédie de l'architecture et de la construction* (1888–92), a twelve volume set containing approximately 4,000 illustrations. He also founded *Construction moderne* (1885), a weekly architectural review. This publication offered the public the opportunity to purchase portfolios similar to the one these illustrations are taken from. This wonderful sourcebook contains a variety of painted designs, including wispy leaves, delicate florals, symmetrical patterns, and geometrics ranging from the Byzantine Era through the reign of Louis XVI.

Bibliographical Note

French Decorative Designs, first published by Dover Publications, Inc. in 2006, contains a new selection of images from *Le Style dans la Peinture Décorative,* originally published by Dujardin & Cie, Éditeurs, Paris, n.d.

Library of Congress Cataloging-in-Publication Data

Planat, P. (Paul), 1839–1911.
    [Style dans la peinture décorative. English. Selections]
    French decorative designs / P. Planat.
        p. cm. — (Dover pictorial archive series)
    A new selection of images from Le style dans la peinture décorative, originally published by Dujardin & Cie.
    ISBN 0-486-45228-X (pbk.)
    1. Decoration and ornament—France—Themes, motives. I. Title.

NK1449.A1P53 2006
745.4—dc22

2006047441

Manufactured in the United States of America
Dover Publications, Inc., 31 East 2nd Street, Mineola, N.Y. 11501

PLATE 1. Byzantine

PLATE 2. Byzantine

PLATE 3. Byzantine

PLATE 4. Byzantine

PLATE 5. Byzantine

PLATE 6. Byzantine

PLATE 7. Byzantine

PLATE 8. Byzantine

PLATE 9. Byzantine

PLATE 10. Byzantine

PLATE 11. Byzantine

PLATE 12. Byzantine

PLATE 13. Byzantine

PLATE 14. Byzantine

PLATE 15. Roman

PLATE 16. Roman

PLATE 17. Roman

PLATE 18. Roman

Plate 19. Roman

PLATE 20. Roman

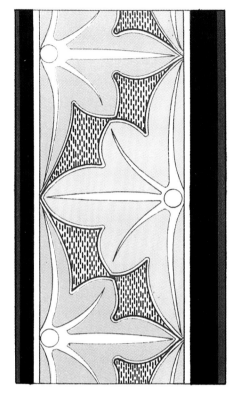

PLATE 21. Roman

PLATE 22. Gothic

PLATE 23. Gothic

PLATE 24. Gothic

Plate 25. Gothic

PLATE 26. Gothic

PLATE 27. Gothic

PLATE 28. Gothic

PLATE 29. Gothic

PLATE 30. Gothic

PLATE 31. Gothic

PLATE 32. Gothic

PLATE 33. Renaissance

PLATE 34. Renaissance

PLATE 35. Renaissance

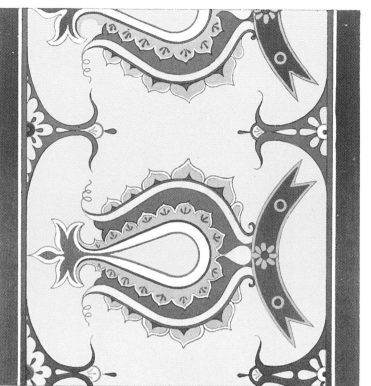

PLATE 36. Renaissance

PLATE 37. Renaissance

PLATE 38. Renaissance (15th to 16th century)

PLATE 39. Renaissance (15th to 16th century)

PLATE 40. Renaissance

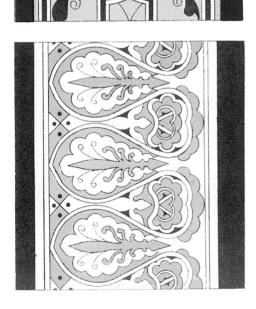

PLATE 41. Renaissance

PLATE 42. Renaissance

PLATE 43. Renaissance

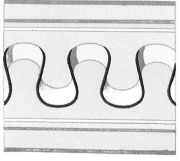

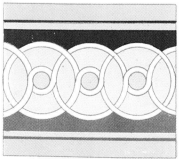

PLATE 44. Late Renaissance (Henry III to Louis XIII)

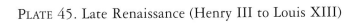

PLATE 45. Late Renaissance (Henry III to Louis XIII)

PLATE 46. Late Renaissance (Henry III to Louis XIII)

PLATE 47. Late Renaissance (Henry III to Louis XIII)

PLATE 48. Late Renaissance (Henry III to Louis XIII)

PLATE 49. Late Renaissance (Henry III to Louis XIII)

PLATE 50. Louis XIV

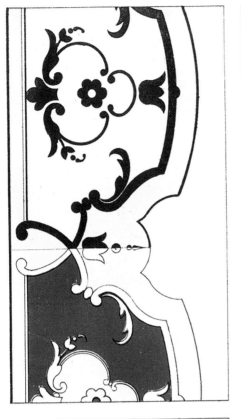

PLATE 51. Louis XIV

PLATE 52. Louis XIV

PLATE 53. Louis XIV

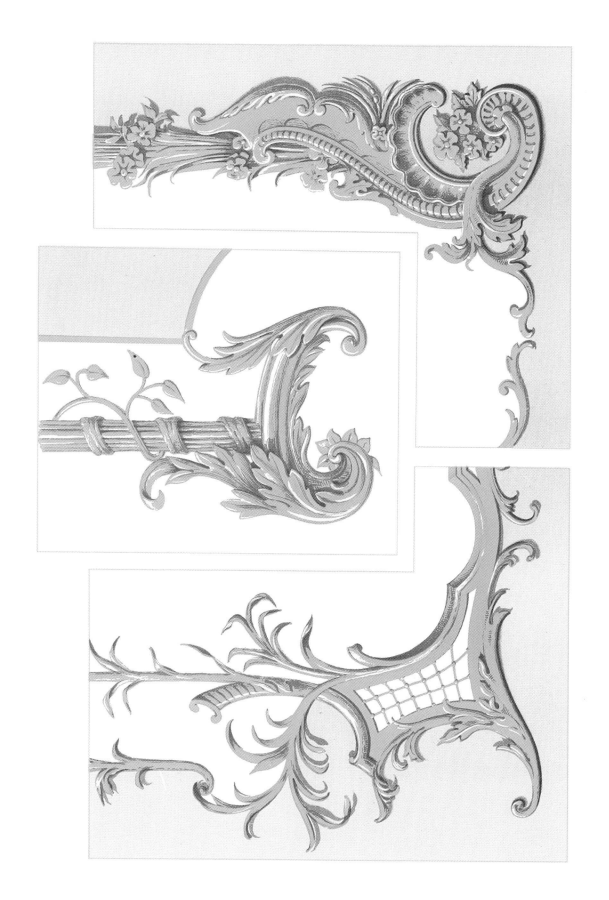

PLATE 54. Louis XV

PLATE 55. Louis XV

PLATE 56. Louis XV

Plate 57. Louis XV

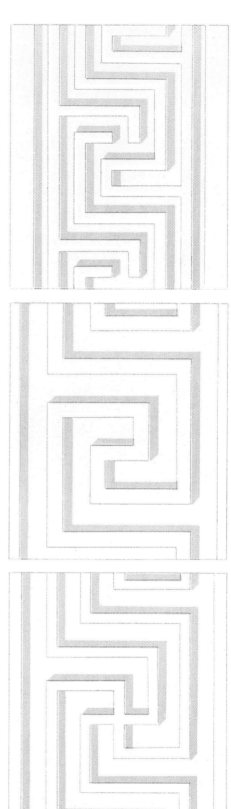

Plate 58. Louis XVI

PLATE 59. Louis XVI

PLATE 60. Louis XVI

PLATE 61. Louis XVI